THE COLLECTED SONGS OF
THEODORE CHANLER

Medium/High Voice and Piano

ED-3887

G. SCHIRMER, Inc.

DISTRIBUTED BY
HAL•LEONARD®
CORPORATION
7777 W. BLUEMOUND RD. P.O. BOX 13819 MILWAUKEE, WI 53213

Preface

Theodore Chanler was one of the finest song composers America produced. He was born in 1902, studied in the 1920's with Nadia Boulanger, and later returned to the United States to teach at the Peabody Conservatory in Baltimore. Chanler settled in Cambridge where he taught theory at the Longy School until his death in 1961. He was an accomplished pianist, mostly in chamber music, and worked occasionally as a music critic and writer on musical subjects. Never a major player on the American musical scene, his reputation rests largely on his song cycle, "Eight Epitaphs."

The first American songs I ever sang in concert were by Chanler. I learned that most wonderful of concert closers, "I Rise When You Enter," and subsequently "Memory," which I still think is one of the most beautiful songs ever written by an American. Because I was young and serious, much like the classical musical climate in the late 1960's, I was hesitant to program "The Doves" (it seemed a lot like popular music to me and I wasn't sure it belonged on a concert program). But I took a chance and sang it a lot because I thought it was wonderful. Audiences seemed to agree with me. I still sing it a lot—it reminds me of popular music and I love it largely for that reason. Chanler had a marvelous way of combining his American sensibilities with what he learned from Boulanger and to create a fresh, sophisticated sound. "The Doves" is a perfect example: it is based on jazz, but Chanler takes it harmonically beyond what popular music did at the time.

I became a big Chanler fan but I soon discovered, to my distress, that almost everything he wrote was out of print or unpublished. When G. Schirmer asked me, many years later, what American songs I wanted to see made available, I was thrilled to put Chanler's at the top of my list. This volume restores to print everything that was published before (except the "Eight Epitaphs" which are available elsewhere) and a number of previously unpublished songs. The score of "Three Husbands" identifies it as Epitaph No. 9 but it was not published as part of the cycle. It can be performed in the cycle (Phyllis Curtin inserted it between nos. four and five) or performed separately.

Chanler was not a prolific composer; he primarily wrote songs, chamber music, and a one-act opera. But the care he lavished on his songs as well as his refinement in both vocal and piano writing embodied his work with a quality that makes up for the lack of quantity. I have been singing some of these pieces for twenty years without ever tiring of them and audiences continue to find them fresh and delightful. I hope, now that this volume is available, that many more singers will share my joy in performing Theodore Chanler.

—PAUL SPERRY

CONTENTS

THE CHILDREN

The Children

Leonard Feeney

Theodore Chanler

Words used by exclusive permission.

And when we grow old-er, what do you sup-pose___ Will be-come of the chil-dren?

sempre f

Will there be chil-dren a-gain, When we who are chil-dren are wo-men and

men? Yes! Sure-ly the world will love

l.h. sf

poco a poco dim.

chil-dren no less; Chil-dren will come when we chil-dren are gone,___

Out of the dark-ness and in - to the dawn,_____ Tak - ing our

plac - es, Bear-ing our bright-ness and light-ness of limbs,_____

____ And our laugh-ter and love in their fac - es.

Once Upon A Time

Leonard Feeney

Theodore Chanler

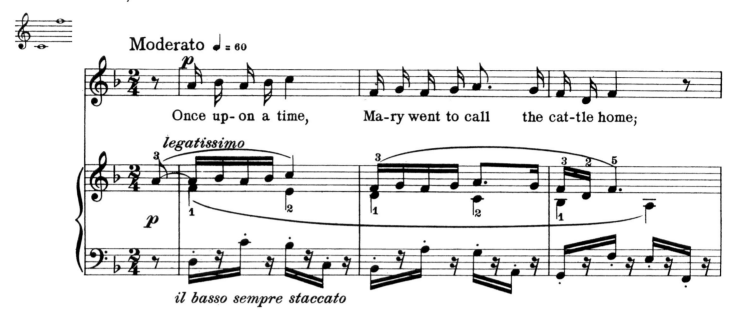

Once up-on a time, Ma-ry went to call the cat-tle home;

Once up-on a time, Ne - ro played a

fid-dle while they burned down Rome;

Words used by exclusive permission.

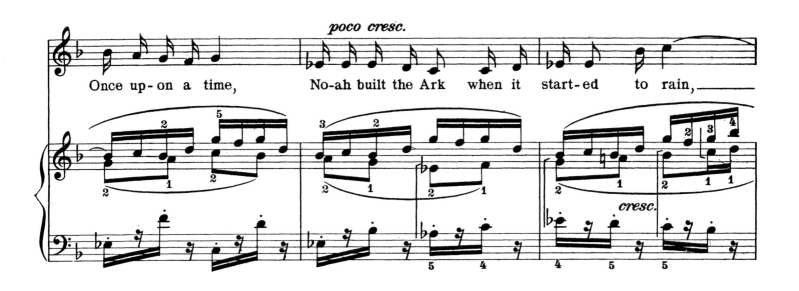

Once up-on a time, No-ah built the Ark when it start-ed to rain,____

____ Laun-ce-lot loved E-laine, Chris-to-pher Co-lum-bus grew

tired of Spain,____ Once up-on a time.____

Once up-on a time, The dish ran a-way with the

spoon;___ Once up-on a time, The but-ter-fly came from the co-

coon, Once up-on a time. There

Wind

Leonard Feeney

Theodore Chanler

Words used by exclusive permission.

And re - turns to a sigh_____ once more.

Wind is the air In your hair,_____ When you stand On the sand By the

shore._____

Wind___ will

shake the lat-tic-es late at night, It will

make the clouds go by; An-y-thing eas-y that's

hard to do, It is pret-ty sure to try:

Blow down a pine, Clothes from a line, Tum-ble a chim-ney top.

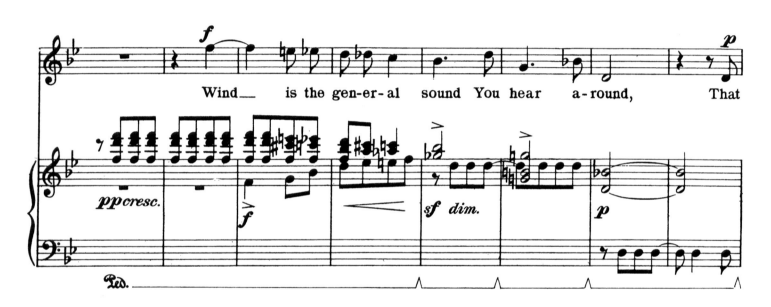

Wind— is the gen-er-al sound You hear a-round, That

sud-den-ly likes to stop.

Lento

Sleep

Leonard Feeney

Theodore Chanler

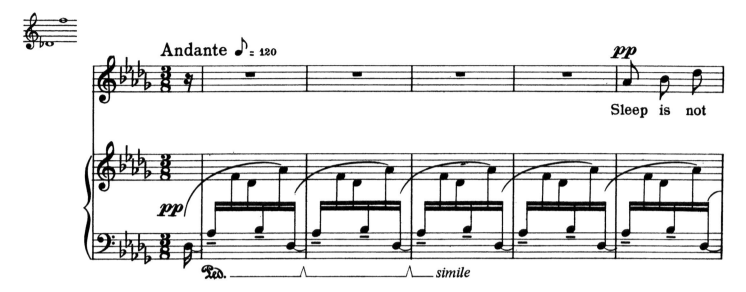

Words used by exclusive permission.

But love it like chil - dren and sleep will come true.

We nev-er go to sleep to dream;____

We go to sleep to go to sleep. Un-

u - su-al as it may seem, We nev - er

senza pedale

spend our time_____ count - ing sheep. A lit-tle

con - fi-dence does the trick When we

pp

To go sail - ing off to a star,

To be bur - ied in a field of hay, To

stop re - mem - ber - ing who we are When we're

fin - ished with our prayers and our play,_____ Af - ter we have

giv-en you   a   good-night   kiss   And   closed   our   eyes   like

this:

Un poco ritenuto

Tempo Iº

It's an aw-ful lot of fun, And it's rest-ful too;

pp cantando

poco cresc.

dim.

pp

Do you see how it's done?___

Do you?___

perdendosi

senza rall.

The Rose

Leonard Feeney

Theodore Chanler

Su - per-im-pose On the

pet-als of a rose An - y hues You choose, And see if you can find What a

gar-den has in mind, That's rose - in-clined.

Go re-

view   your heart's hor - ti - cul - ture,   A-mid   sun - light and shad-ows and

show'rs;   Take a   book That you took From the   li-bra-ry, and look Up   the

cresc.

p subito

fas - ci-nat - ing his-to-ry of flow'rs.

p subito

Grandma

Leonard Feeney

Theodore Chanler

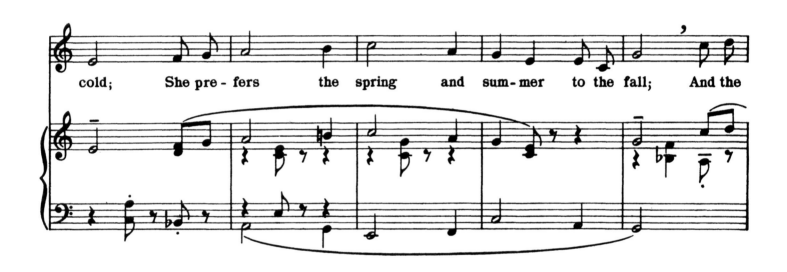

Words used by exclusive permission.

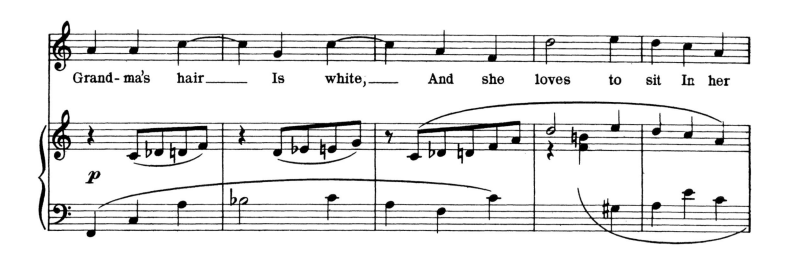

Grand-ma's hair___ Is white,___ And she loves to sit In her

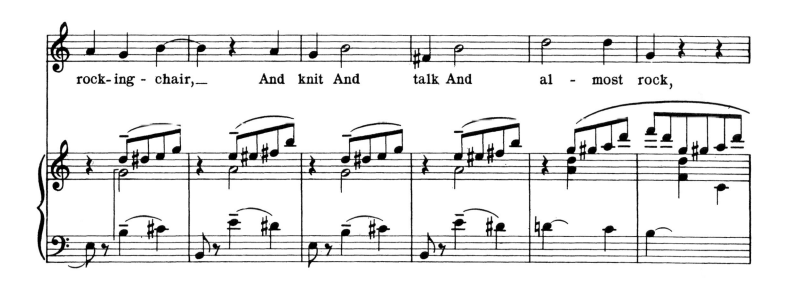

rock-ing-chair,___ And knit And talk And al - most rock,

sempre **pp**

And see you dim - ly___ with her poor eye - sight.

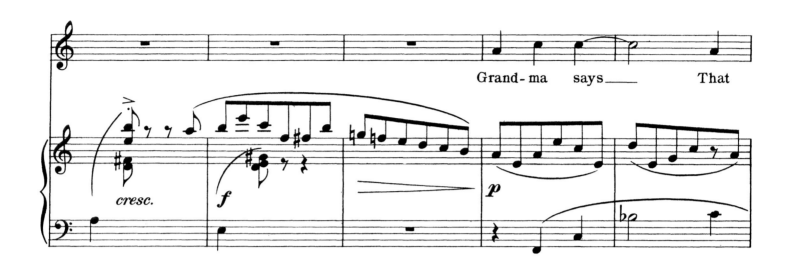

Grand - ma says___ That

God Is good, But that His ways Are odd And can - not be

al - ways___ Un - der - stood. But af - ter she has

tak - en a cook-ie from the shelf, And giv-en it to you And

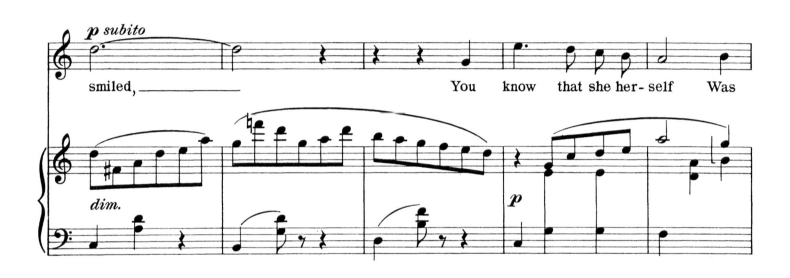

smiled, _____ You know that she her-self Was

once a lit-tle child, And had a grand-ma too. _____

Spick and Span

Leonard Feeney

Theodore Chanler

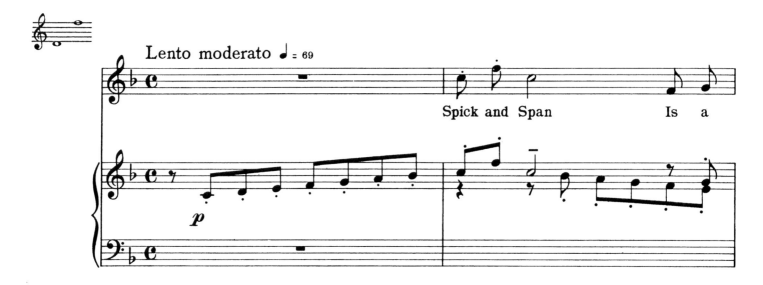

Spick and Span Is a

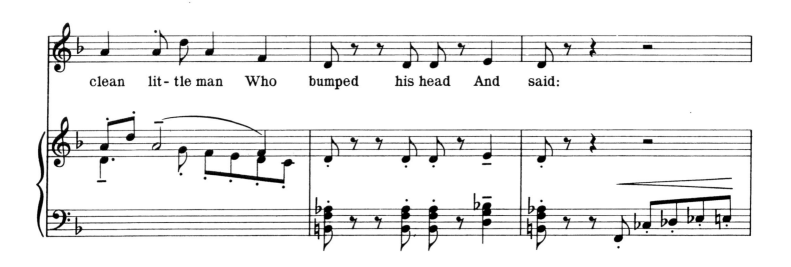

clean lit-tle man Who bumped his head And said:

"Black and blue, I know you!"

Words used by exclusive permission.

Moo is a Cow

Leonard Feeney

Theodore Chanler

Words used by exclusive permission.

Peek-a-boo Is may-be I don't see you, But I'm
sure you can't see me; Splash is a stone When a
big one's thrown In a riv-er or lake or sea.

Hush is your lip When your fin - ger-tip Says you should-n't make a

sound; Hop is a toad Right a-

cross the road, With-out stop-ping to look a - round;

Pit - a - pat is rain On the win-dow-pane; Buzz-a-

buzz a bus - y bee; Creak is a stair, When you

ask "Who's there?" And there's no one to say "It's me".

Tick is a clock, Click is a lock Af - ter you've closed the door;

p molto leggero

dim.

And a soft tip - toe Is to let you know You have fal - len a - sleep once

pp

more.

cantando

mp dolce

Bounce is a ball Up a-gainst a wall, When you've

giv-en it a throw. Rip is a tear In a

thing you wear, That your moth-er will want to sew; Rub-a-

dub - dub - dub Is a drum-mer-boy, When a band goes march-ing

by; Twin - kle's a bright Lit-tle

star at night, Or a fun-ny look in your eye.

One of Us

Leonard Feeney

Theodore Chanler

Hus-bands and wives! Are we not your lit-tle lives?

Fa-thers and moth-ers! Who but we will be your oth-ers?

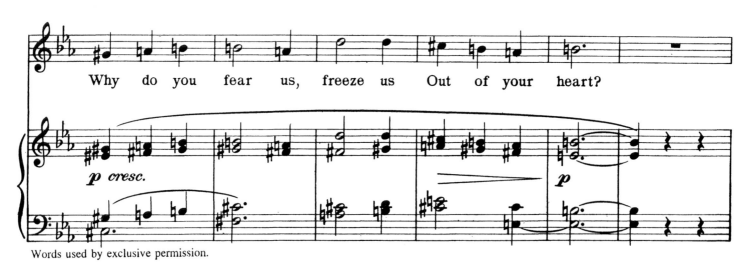

Why do you fear us, freeze us Out of your heart?

Words used by exclusive permission.

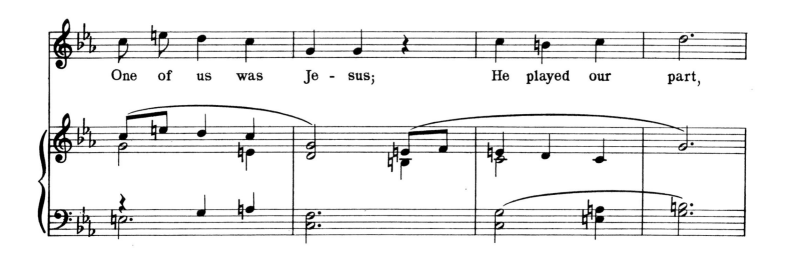

One of us was Je - sus; He played our part,

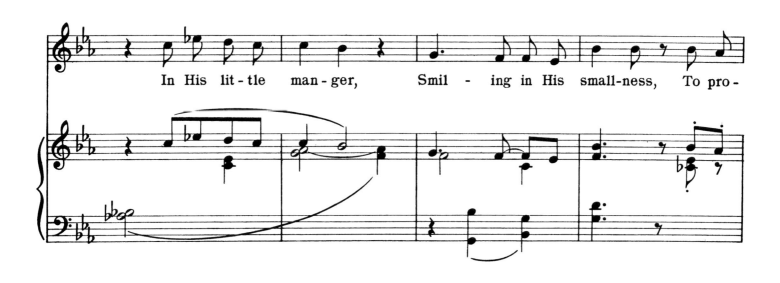

In His lit - tle man - ger, Smil - ing in His small-ness, To pro -

tect us from the dan - ger Of noth - ing - at - all - ness.

One of us was God. Has this not been told a - broad, To

some by song, To some by star?___ Then when will we be

known For what we are?___

FOUR RHYMES FROM PEACOCK PIE

The Ship of Rio

Walter de la Mare

Theodore Chanler

Poem from Collected Poems by Walter de la Mare, by permission of Henry Holt & Co., publishers.

quar-ter to ca-boose, there weren't a stitch of cal-i-co to

breech 'em— tight or loose. From spar to deck, from deck to keel, from

bar-na-cle to shroud, there weren't one pair of reach-me-downs to

all that jab-ber-ing crew. But

was-n't it a glad-some sight, when roared the deep sea gales, to

see them reef her fore and aft, a - swinging by their tails!

Oh, was-n't it a glad-some sight, when glass-y calm____

____ did come, to see them squat-ting, tai - lor -wise, a -

Old Shellover

Walter de la Mare

Theodore Chanler

Poem from Collected Poems by Walter de la Mare, by permission of Henry Holt & Co., publishers.

Cake and Sack

Walter de la Mare

Theodore Chanler

Poem from Collected Poems by Walter de la Mare, by permission of Henry Holt & Co., publishers.

50

Tillie

Walter de la Mare

Theodore Chanler

Poem from Peacock Pie, by permission of Henry Holt & Co., publishers.

There, as she yawned And yawn wide— did she, float - ed some seed Down her gull - e (ee) - t (tee);

poco rit.

a tempo

And look you

once, and look you twice, poor Old Til-lie was

gone in a trice.

But oh, when the wind do a-moan - ing

THREE EPITAPHS

Mistress Hew

Walter de la Mare

Theodore Chanler

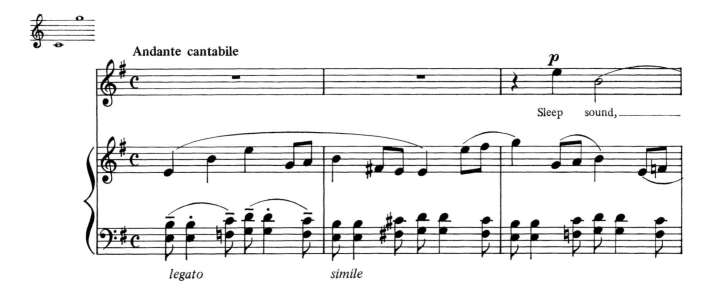

Your own ____ hands   did nour-ish;   And man-y's the child By their

beau - ty be-guiled   They prat-tle and play   Till ____ night call _____ them a -

way;   In ____

A Shepherd

Walter de la Mare

Theodore Chanler

Shep - herd, Ned Vaughan, 'Neath this Tomb - stone do bide,

His Crook in his hand, And his Dog him be - side.

Poem from Collected Poems by Walter de la Mare, by permission of Henry Holt & Co., publishers.

A One-eyed Tailor

Walter de la Mare

Theodore Chanler

Here's an old Tai - lor, rest his eye:

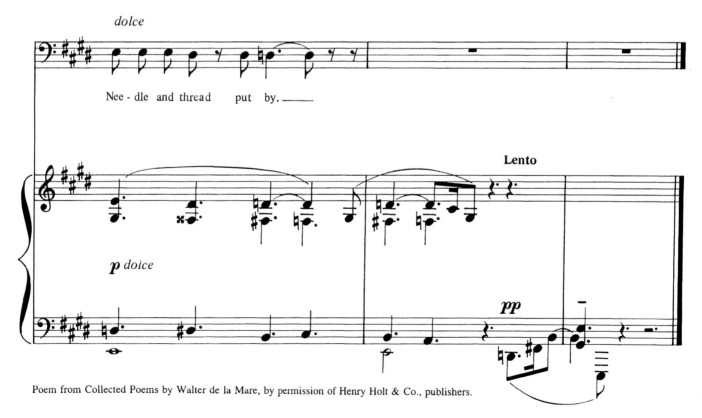

Nee - dle and thread put by.

Poem from Collected Poems by Walter de la Mare, by permission of Henry Holt & Co., publishers.

THREE MONTHS AND A RABBIT

to Louise Sargent

1. April

Daniel Sargent

to Maria

Theodore Chanler

Words used by exclusive permission.

glides and spins.

Lead her through a veil of rain _____ Where cre -

a - tion starts a - gain. _____

A - pril,

meno f

p

A - pril, lead her feet Where the vi - o - lets are sweet.

Lead her where the an - gels glide

Down the sun - beams _____ to her

side. _____

2. May

to my mother

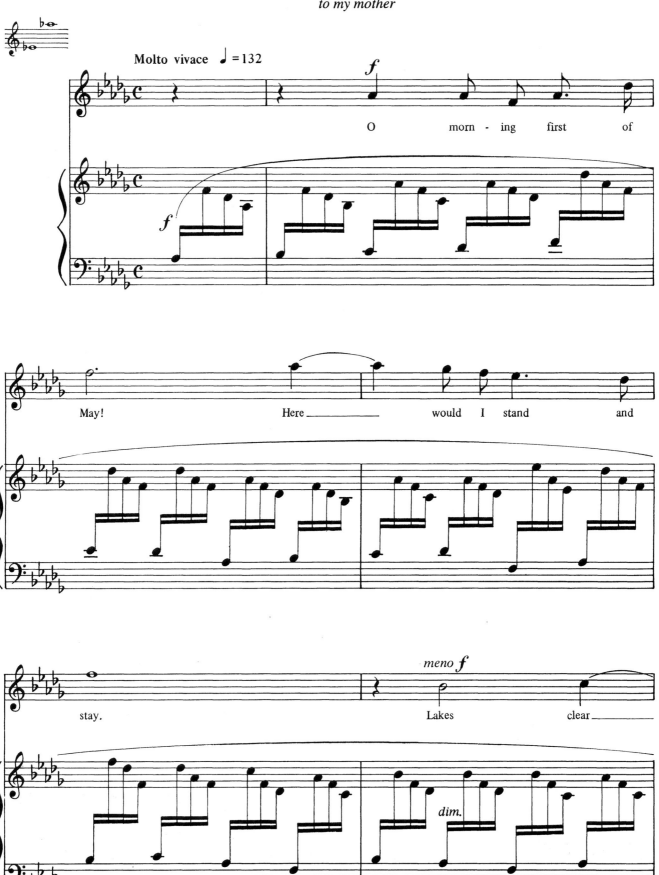

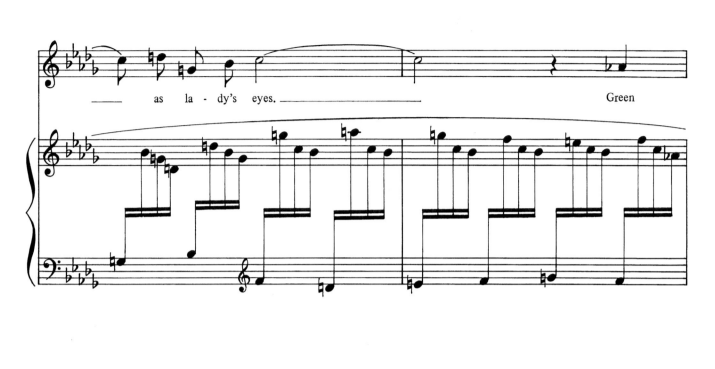

as la - dy's eyes. _____ Green

wil - lows, ____ hap - py skies.

And then the rush - ing rain: Old

f

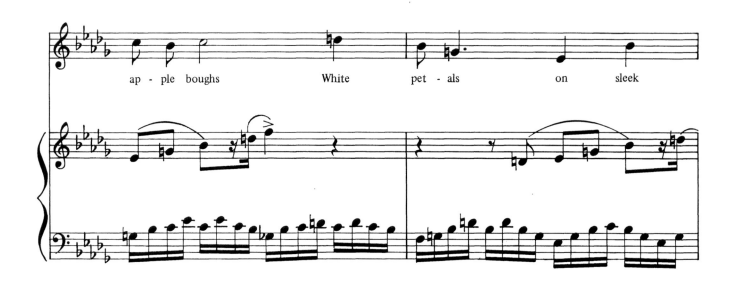

ap - ple boughs   White   pet - als   on   sleek

cows.

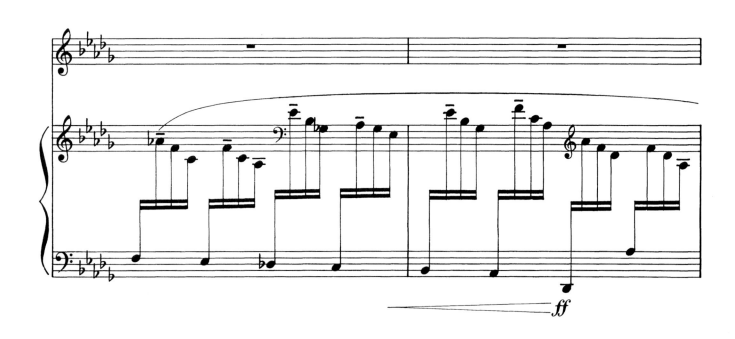

O morn - ing first of May! O

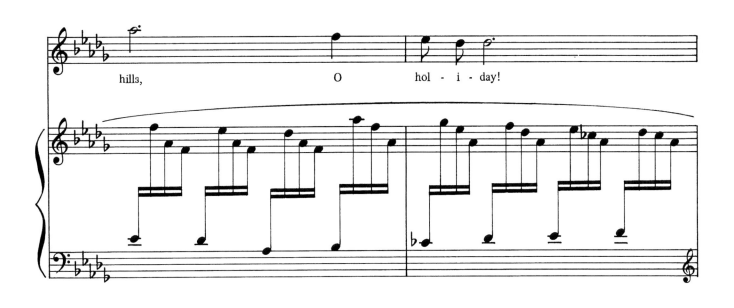

hills, O hol - i - day!

Let sweep - ing swal - lows chase

Blue winds on the stream's face.

The dan - de - li - ons know which

ff

mf

f

meno f subito

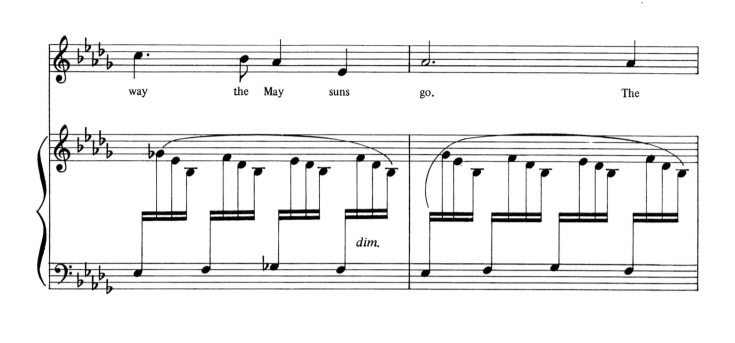

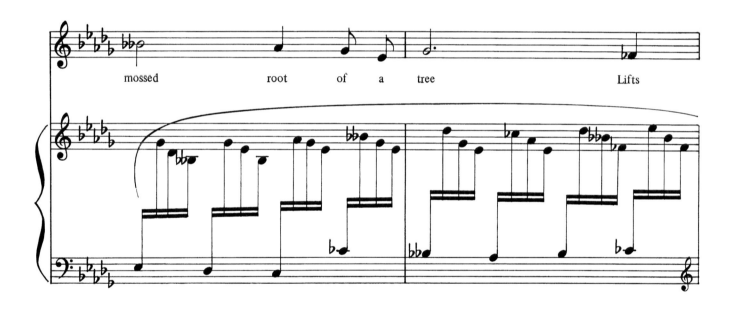

74

3. June

to Eva Gauthier

Andantino

June is too rich. I do not dare Sing a - bout June.

p legato

She is too fair. She has too man - y frogs at night

p

poco cresc.

Sing - ing with their or - ches - tral might. She has too man - y

cresc.

p

Copyright © 1994 by G. Schirmer, Inc. (ASCAP) New York, NY
International Copyright Secured. All Rights Reserved.
**Warning: Unauthorized reproduction of this publication is
prohibited by Federal law and subject to criminal prosecution.**

She has too man - y

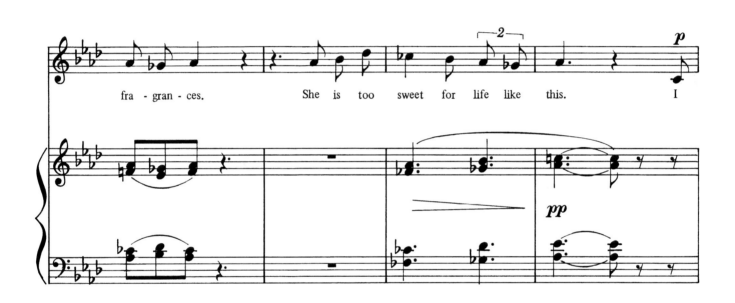

fra - gran - ces. She is too sweet for life like this. I

feel in June like some cleft stone In which the sword - ferns

78

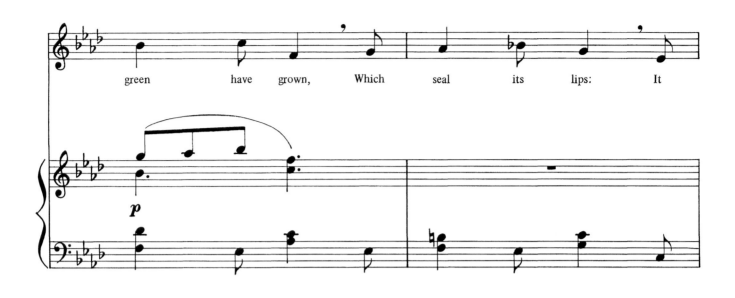

green have grown, Which seal its lips: It

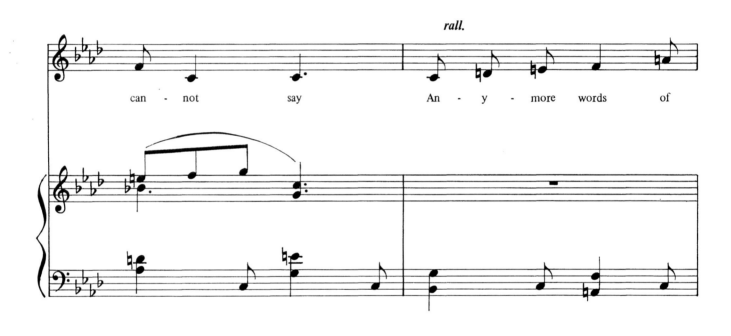

can - not say An - y - more words of

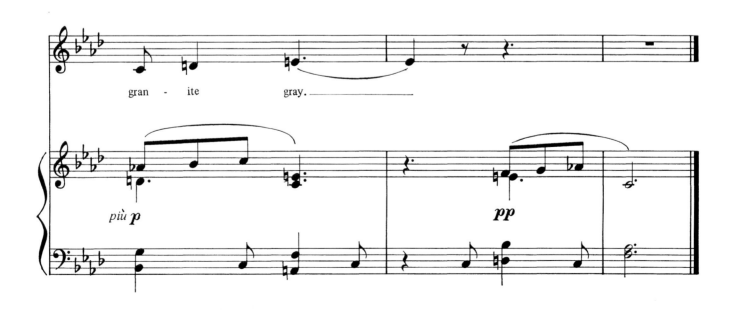

gran - ite gray.

4. Cottony Cottony

to Maria

Dear lit - tle rab - bit, cot - ton - y, cot - ton - y,

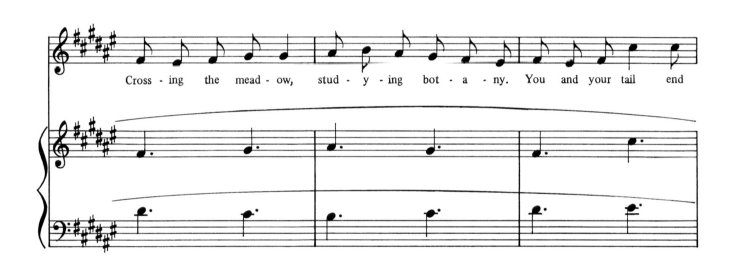

Cross - ing the mead - ow, stud - y - ing bot - a - ny. You and your tail end

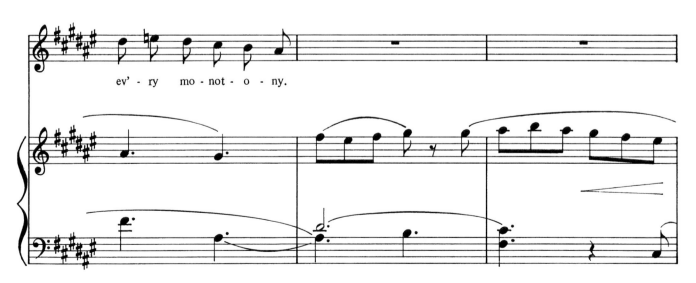

ev' - ry mo - not - o - ny.

Words used by exclusive permission.

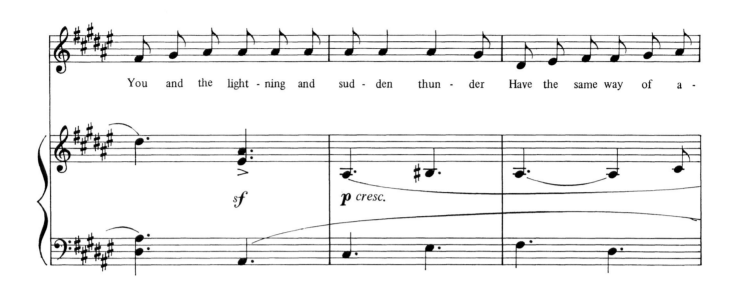

You and the light-ning and sud-den thun-der Have the same way of a-

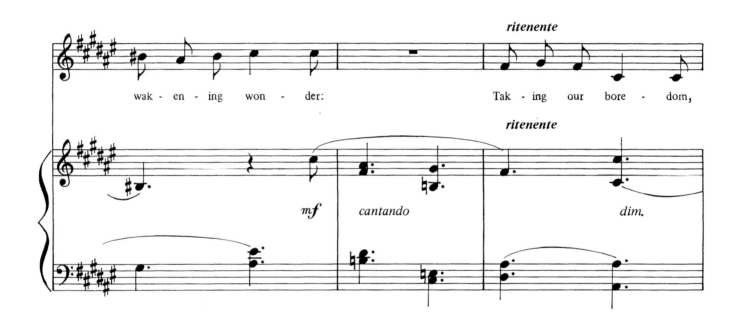

wak-en-ing won-der: Tak-ing our bore-dom,

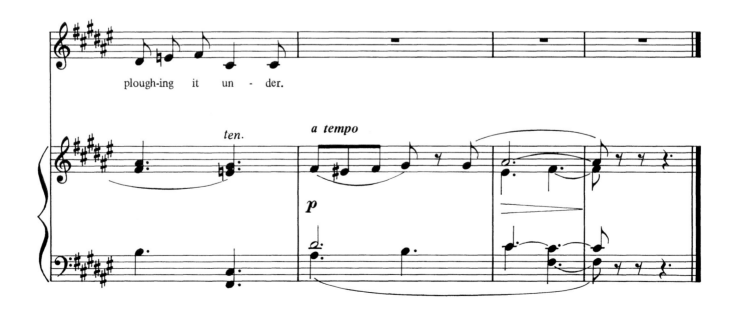

plough-ing it un-der.

My Hands are Empty

Purchit Swami

Theodore Chanler

emp - ty,   All   that   talk   a - mounts   to   noth - ing.

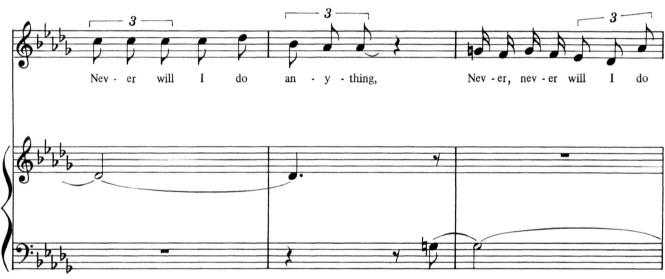

Nev - er   will   I   do   an - y - thing,   Nev - er, nev - er will   I   do

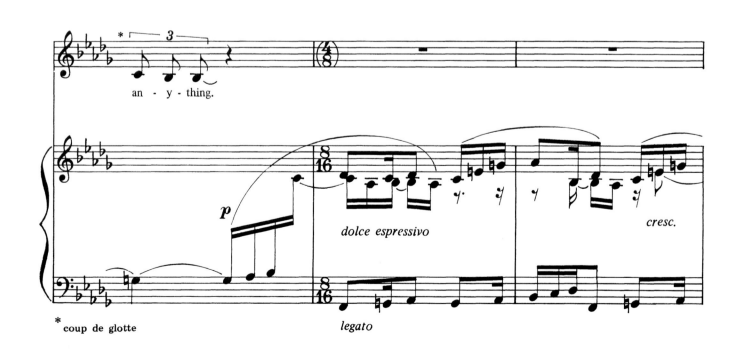

an - y - thing.

*coup de glotte

dolce espressivo

legato

cresc.

Hav - ing been com - mand - ed to woo Thee I should keep my-self wide a -

wake

Or else sleep ___ a - way my life.

I am un - fit to do the first, But I can

sleep   with   o - pen   eyes   And   I   can   al -

- ways   pre - tend   to   laugh

And   I   can   weep   for   the

state I   am   in.

Tempo I

dolce cantabile

p   *pp*   *p*

legato

cresc.

poco rit.

dim.

pp   *p*

But my   laugh   has gone for

good,   And gone the charm of   tears.

Voyage in Provence

Archibald MacLeish

Theodore Chanler

Cradle Song

William Blake

Theodore Chanler

Sweet   sleep   with soft

dream. _____

Weave   thy   brows   an

p poco sostenuto

rall. e dim.

pp [a tempo]

pp

in - - - fant

crown.

pp

stretto

rall. e dim.

pp

Meet Doctor Livermore

Leonard Feeney

Theodore Chanler

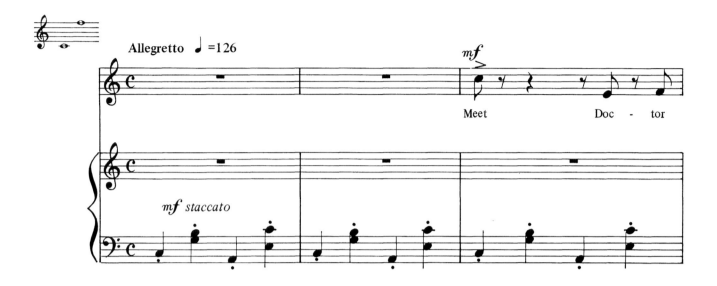

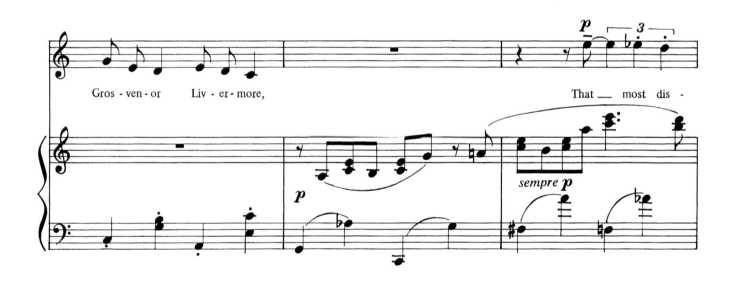

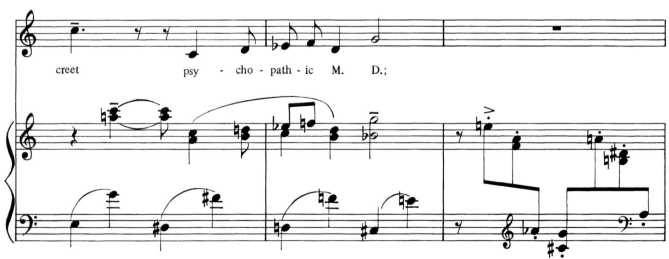

Words used by exclusive permission.

Greet him, and tell him what you most ab - hor, ___ And let him look at you sus -

pi - cious - ly. He'll be un sur - prised as an - y - thing, He will

al - ways have known you of yore; And a nice lit - tle vice, Dis -

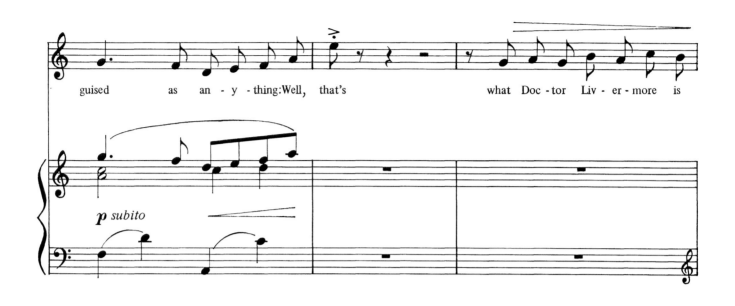

guised as an-y-thing: Well, that's what Doc-tor Liv-er-more is

p subito

for.

pp *mf*

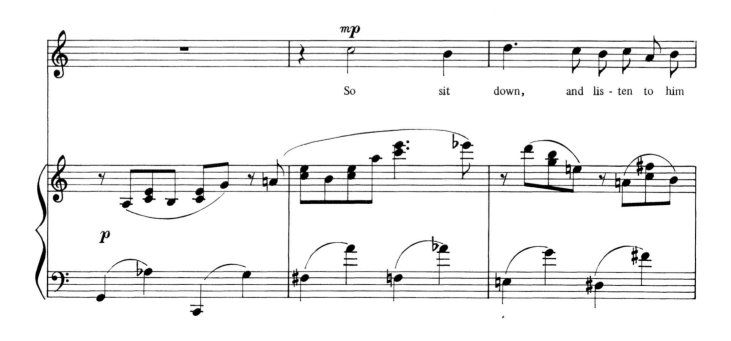

So sit down, and lis-ten to him

mp

p

chat - ter, The while he tells you what to tell him is the mat - ter; And if you

cresc.

fear _____ what he's a - fraid that you have got: If you're a

split per - son al - i - ty nut, A com -

plete - ly un - mo - ti - va - ted mut; If your

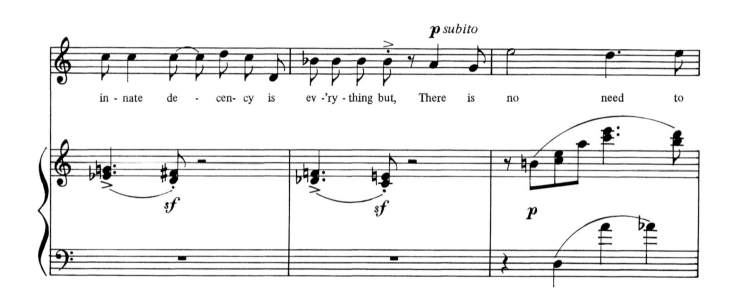

in - nate de - cen - cy is ev - 'ry - thing but, There is no need to

shiv - er more, Once you meet Doc - tor Liv - er - more.

The Doves

Leonard Feeney

Theodore Chanler

Allegretto molto moderato

mezza voce

The doves ____ they fly ____ to the moon-lit elms and cry: Tick - i - ta coo! Tick - i - ta coo! The whole night through. ____

p staccato

Words used by exclusive permission.

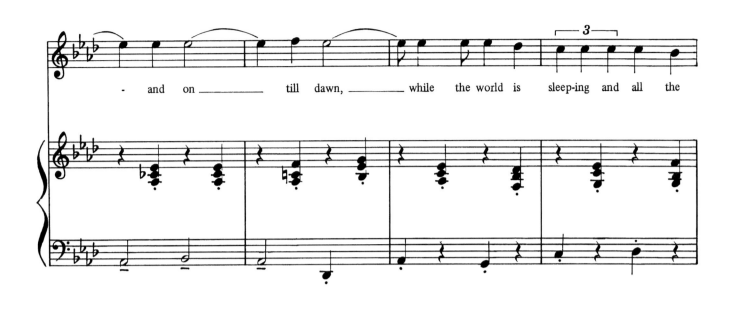

- and on ____ till dawn, ____ while the world is sleep-ing and all the

oth - er birds ____ are too, They wake ____ and shake the

sil - ver - y leaves with a strain that is nev - er old, ____ and nev - er

new.

There's snow _____ up - on their fea - thers, _____ but their

breasts are full of flame.

The sea - sons change, _____ but still their mel - o - dy stays the

same: Tick - i - ta coo! Tick - i - ta - coo! Ev - er soft and

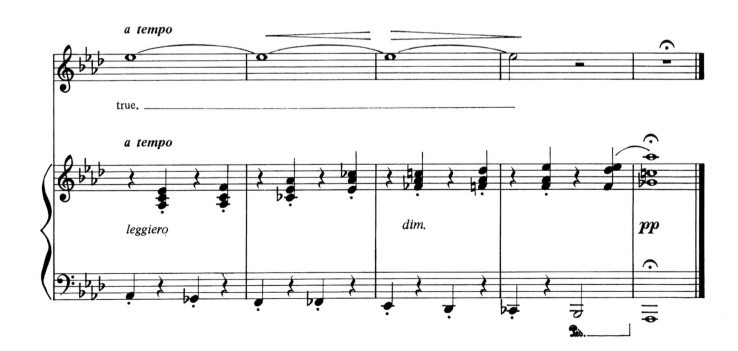

true. _____

Memory

William Blake

Theodore Chanler

fish for fan-cies as they pass With-in the wa-t'ry glass.

I'll drink of the clear stream, And hear the lin - net's song; And

there I'll lie and dream The day a - long: ___ And, when night comes, I'll go To

plac-es fit for woe, __ Walking a-long the darkened val - ley With si - - - -

- - - lent Mel - an - choly.

These, My Ophelia

Archibald MacLeish

Theodore Chanler

And our yes-ter-day___ O___ my O-phel-ia___

Shall be the eve-ning star For some

earth that turns___ from Arc-tur-us When we no long-er my O-phel-ia

crescendo

Come here to the oak a-bove the sea___

poco rit.

diminuendo

The Policeman in the Park

Leonard Feeney

Theodore Chanler

Words used by exclusive permission.

lice - man   in   the park.   When the

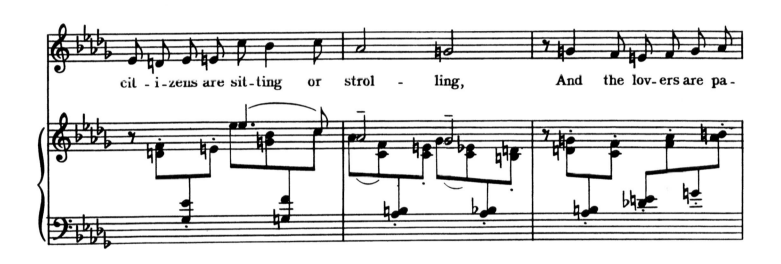

cit - i - zens are sit - ting   or   strol - ling,   And   the lov - ers are pa -

trol - ling   in   the dark,

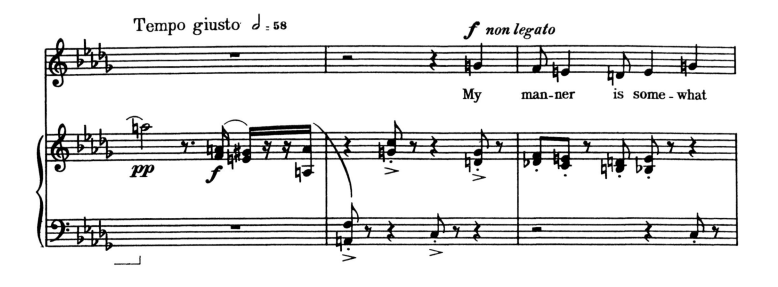

My man-ner is some-what

dis-tant and se-vere; Here and there I make a re-mark.

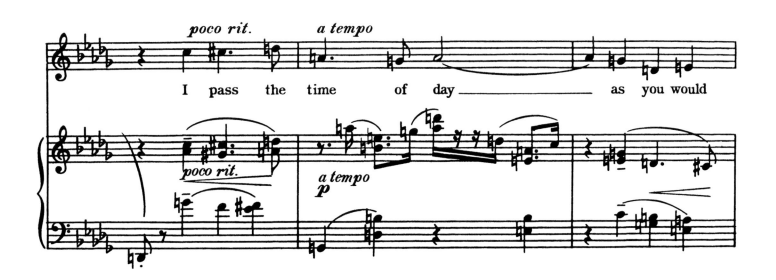

I pass the time of day _____ as you would

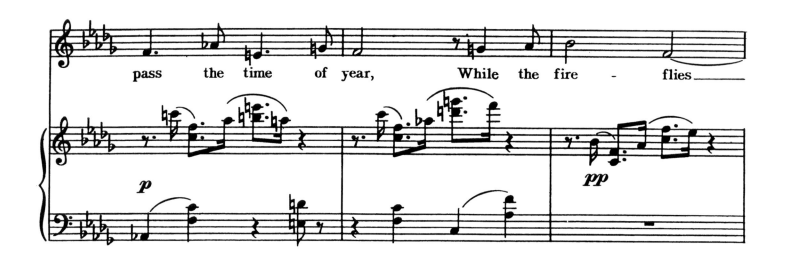

pass the time of year, While the fire - flies___

___ con - tin - ue to spark.

With the earth be - low me, And the air a-round and a - bove me, With

few who per-son-al-ly know me, And no one to love me, I — am the po-

Più mosso ♩ = 64

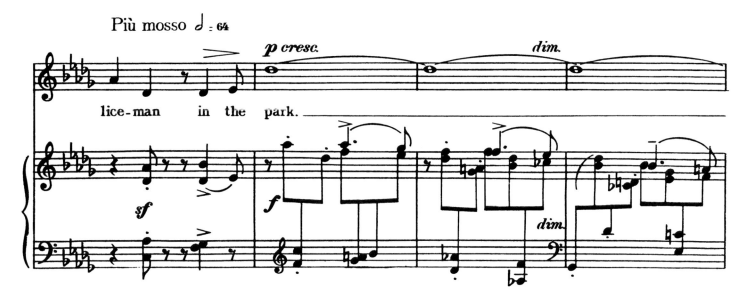

lice-man in the park.

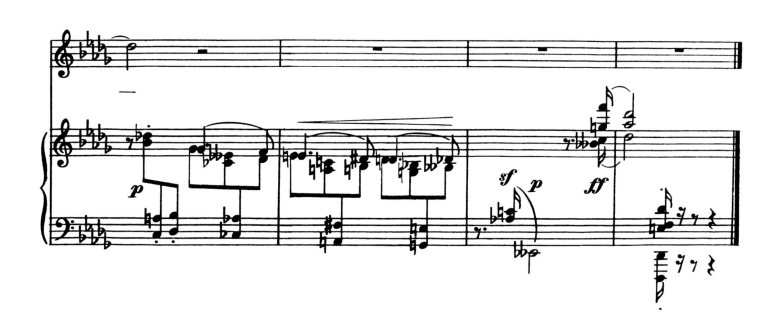

The Lamb

William Blake

Theodore Chanler

I Rise When You Enter

Leonard Feeney

Theodore Chanler

Words used by exclusive permission.

Of at - trac - tion I tell you, if an - y - thing's true, _____

You're the ab - - so - lute cen - ter.

I take off my

hat When I ride with you down _____ on the lift

You are so won - der - ful, what shall I say? ———

Shall I tell ———— you a sto - ry

Of a knight and a maid and the old fash-ioned way

*Small notes *ad lib*.

to Eva Gauthier

O Mistress Mine

William Shakespeare

Theodore Chanler

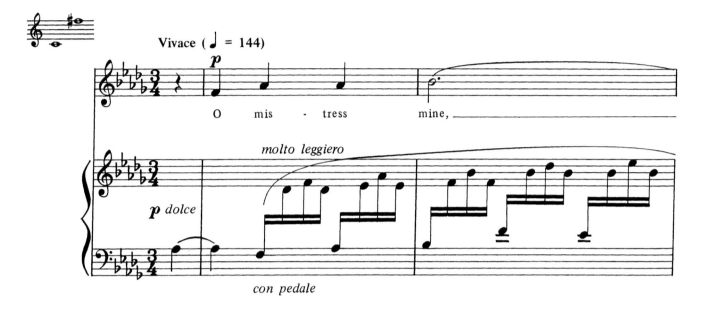

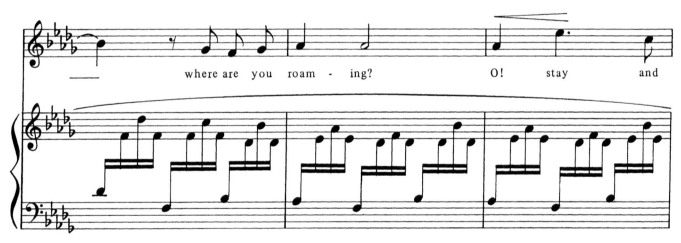

That can sing _____ both high _____ and low _____

poco rit.

p

Trip no fur - ther, pret - ty sweet - ing;

a tempo

p grazioso

Jour - ney's end in lov - ers'

pp

130

Three Husbands
(Epitaph No. 9)

Walter de la Mare

Theodore Chanler

Here lies my hus-bands; One, Two, Three: Dumb as men ev-er could

wish to be. As for my fourth, well,

Copyright © 1962 by G. Schirmer, Inc. (ASCAP) New York, NY

Praise be God, He bides for a lit-tle a-bove___

giocoso
f sub.

_p_

___ the sod.

But his wits

dolce

tremolando

be-ing weak___ and his eye - balls dim.

Heav'n speed at last I'll wear weeds for him.

p sempre

molto leggero

La la   la la la   la la la

Thom-as,   John,   Hen-ry,   were these   three's

pp

f

ff

f

names.___   And   to make things

f

dim. subito

f

ti - dy   I adds   his   James.

non rit.